Hufnagel Pütz Rafaelian

Editorial

Die fünf hier dargestellten, realisierten oder kurz vor Fertigstellung stehenden Bauten sind deckungsgleich mit dem Werkverzeichnis des Berliner Architektenteams Karl Hufnagel, Peter Pütz und Michael Rafaelian seit 1992: fünf ausgeführte Bauten und etliche Wettbewerbsbeiträge, viele davon mit dem ersten, zweiten oder dritten Preis ausgezeichnet.
Lese ich die minutiösen Baubeschreibungen und Lösungsherleitungen, dann schwingt hier Ernsthaftigkeit, Beharrlichkeit und eine Vorliebe für städtebauliche Fragen mit. Wir erkennen den respektvollen und sorgfältigen Umgang mit dem Bestand, den es vorerst zu reparieren, zu ordnen und zu ergänzen gilt. Im Vordergrund steht nicht ein architektonischer Ausdruck oder das Setzen von Monumenten, sondern der Umgang mit der Realität, mit der Stadt als einem vorhandenen Organismus. Es gilt, die Qualitäten der Stadt freizulegen und das Neue mit ihr gewinnbringend zu verweben.
Diese Vorliebe für das Städtebauliche finden wir schliesslich auch in jedem der architektonischen Entwürfe. Bei der Sporthalle zur Max-Taut-Schule in Berlin beispielsweise finden wir eine in allen Details präzise Setzung der Baukörper und eine beispielhafte subtile Verzahnung von Innen- und Aussenräumen, im Garderobentrakt etwa durch eine innere Fortsetzung der äusseren städtebaulichen Struktur. Oder auch beim Kunstmuseum in Leipzig, wo das Wesen des Bauwerks weniger in der äusseren Gestalt oder in der Fassadengestaltung liegt, sondern vielmehr in der inneren Konzeption. Die in der Vertikalen wie in der Horizontalen verschränkten mächtigen Räume schaffen eine eigentliche wundersame Stadt im Gebäude. Die Anlage entspricht weder der klassischen geschossweisen Organisation wie sie noch in den 80er Jahren von Remy Zaugg proklamiert wurde, noch ist sie mit der opulenten Raum- und Formenvielfalt zahlreicher jüngerer Museumsbauten mit dekonstruktivistischem Ansatz vergleichbar. Der Besucher bewegt sich hier in einem symphonischen Raumorganismus, worin sich Kunst- und Raumerlebnis gegenseitig stimulieren und intensivieren. Die architektonischen Entscheide sind dabei nicht von malerischer Natur. Sie vereinigen vielmehr das Pragmatische mit der Ästhetik. Sie finden im Notwendigen das darin angelegte Ästhetische, die darin angelegte Schönheit.

Luzern, im April 2011, Heinz Wirz

Editorial notes

The five buildings presented in this volume, some of which have already been built, others which have almost been completed, are congruent with the catalogue of works created since 1992 by the team of architects from Berlin: Karl Hufnagel, Peter Pütz and Michael Rafaelian: five constructed buildings and numerous competition entries, many of which have been awarded with a first, second or third prize.
On reading the meticulous building specifications and proposed solutions, I find they resonate with sincerity, persistence and a fondness for urban planning issues. One can perceive a respectful and careful approach to the existing building, and the initial task of repairing, structuring and supplementing it. The emphasis is not on architectural expression or the creation of a monument but a way of dealing with reality, with the city as an existing organism. Here, the task at hand is to uncover the qualities of the city and interweave them with the new aspects in a way that is beneficial.
This fondness for urban development can be found ultimately in each of the architectural designs. In the case of the sports hall for the Max-Taut school in Berlin for example in the precise alignment of the building structure and an exemplary, subtle interlocking of the interior and exterior space, achieved in the cloakroom tract by the continuation of the outer urban structure in the interior. Or also in the case of the Kunstmuseum in Leipzig, where the essence of the building structure can be found less in the design of the exterior or the facade but to a much greater extent in the concept for the interior. The rooms, which have a strong presence and are interlocked on a vertical and horizontal level, create a wonderful city within a building. The facility neither corresponds with the classical organisation of a building into storeys as proclaimed by Remy Zaugg in the 80s, nor is it comparable with the abundant diversity of space and forms found in numerous more recent museum buildings that take a deconstructivist approach. The visitor moves within a symphonic spatial organism, in which the experience of art and space is mutually stimulating and inspiring. The architectural decisions here are not of a painterly nature. They consolidate to a much greater extent the pragmatic with the aesthetic. They seek out the aesthetic that lies within the essential, the beauty inherent within it.

Lucerne, in April 2011, Heinz Wirz

De aedibus international

**Hufnagel Pütz Rafaelian
Berlin**

Quart Verlag Luzern

Hufnagel Pütz Rafaelian
3. Band der Reihe De aedibus international/Volume 3 of the series De aedibus international

Herausgeber/Edited by: Heinz Wirz, Luzern
Konzept/Concept: Hufnagel Pütz Rafaelian, Berlin; Heinz Wirz
Textbeitrag/Contributions: Karl Hufnagel, Berlin
Objekttexte/Describtion of the projects: Hufnagel Pütz Rafaelian
Vorwort/Foreword: Heinz Wirz
Übersetzung aus dem Deutschen/English Translation: Gillian Morris, Berlin
Fotos/Photos: Christian Gahl, Berlin S. 38–40, 41 u.; Archiv Hufnagel Pütz Rafaelian, Berlin S. 7 u., 10, 11 u., 15 l. u., 17 l. u., 18 l. u., 20, 21, 32, 34, 35, 41 o., 45 u., 46, 47, 49 o. r.; Werner Huthmacher, Berlin S. 12 o., 13–15 r. u., 18 l. u., 19, 22, 24–26, 27 u., 28–31; Linus Lintner, Berlin S. 16, 18 l. o.; M. Ulrich, Berlin S. 36, 37
Renderings: Hinrichs Grafikdesign, Berlin S. 9, 42
Grafische Umsetzung/Graphic Design: Quart Verlag, Luzern
Lithos: Printeria, Luzern
Druck/Printing: Engelberger Druck AG, Stans

© Copyright 2011
Quart Verlag Luzern, Heinz Wirz
Alle Rechte vorbehalten/All rights reserved
ISBN 978-3-03761-026-8

Quart Verlag GmbH
Denkmalstrasse 2, CH-6006 Luzern
books@quart.ch, www.quart.ch

Printed in Switzerland

6	Autonomie und Bindung/Autonomy and Connectivity Karl Hufnagel

Realisierte Bauten/Constructed Buildings

10	Thermalbad und Therapiezentrum/Hot Springs and Therapy Centre, Bad Saarow
16	Studentenwohnheime/Student Halls of Residence, Brandenburg
22	Museum der Bildenden Künste/Museum of Fine Arts, Leipzig
32	Sporthalle Max-Taut-Schule/Sports Hall Max-Taut-School, Berlin
42	Erweiterung/Extension Kunsthalle Bremen

Geplante Projekte/Planned Projects

50	Der Marstallplatz als Komplettierung der Münchner Residenz/The Marstallplatz as the Completion of a Residence in Munich
52	Erweiterung der Museumsinsel/Extension of Museumsinsel, Berlin
54	Humboldt-Forum «Stadtschloss», Berlin/Humboldt-Forum City Palace (Stadtschloss), Berlin
56	Werkverzeichnis/List of Works
62	Biografien, Auszeichnungen, Bibliografie Biographies, Awards, Bibliography

Autonomie und Bindung
Karl Hufnagel

Autonomy and Connectivity
Karl Hufnagel

Im Diskurs des Architekturschaffens, zwischen kontextuellem Bauen und autonomer Form, wird in unserer in fast zwei Jahrzehnten entstandenen Arbeit abseits vordergründiger Formalismen und Ideologien eine durchgehend konzeptuelle Entwurfshaltung sichtbar. Der Weg vom Kontext zur autonomen Form, mit Berührungspunkten zur zeitgenössischen Kunst, findet seine Entsprechung in der Ausarbeitung der Entwürfe von der äusseren Erscheinung, der Disposition im Stadtraum bis hinein in die architektonischen Räume und die Materialität der Architektur. Unabhängig davon, ob es sich um kleinmassstäbliche Architekturaufgaben oder den Masterplan für die langfristige städtebauliche Entwicklung urbaner Quartiere handelt, liegen den Arbeiten verbindende Strategien zugrunde. Unsere Projekte stehen exemplarisch für eine Auffassung, die Architektur und Städtebau dezidiert als Einheit sieht und dies mit einer umfassenden Reflexion über das Verhältnis von Architektur und Stadt verbindet.

Die städtebaulichen Arbeiten formulieren strukturelle Lösungen für begrenzte Areale und setzen gleichzeitig architektonisch das Bild einer veränderten Realität in die Welt. In stadtbildprägenden autonomen Baufeldern, die ihre bauliche Form aus der Interpretation des Ortes ableiten, werden Strategien angelegt, die heute anstelle einer verloren gegangenen verbindlichen Konvention das einheitliche Wachsen von Stadt ermöglichen. Analog zu dieser Betrachtungsweise bilden bei Interventionen von architekto-

In the architectural production discourse, between contextual construction and autonomous form, a consistent conceptual design approach becomes evident in the works created over a period of almost two decades, works that do not conform to predominant formalism or ideology. The progression from the concept to the autonomous form that touches on aspects of contemporary art, corresponds to the development of design concepts for the outer appearance of a building, its positioning within the urban space, right through to the nature of the architectural spaces and the construction materials. Irrespective of whether we are dealing with small-scale architectural tasks or the master plan for the long-term town planning and development of urban quarters, the works are based on connective strategies. Our projects are exemplary for an approach that views architecture and urban planning very much as one unit, while at the same time taking the relationship between architecture and the city into account.

The urbanistic works convey structural solutions for defined sites and at the same time architecturally put forth the concept of a changed reality. Strategies are applied to autonomous building plots that have a formative effect on the appearance of the city and whose architecture is based on an interpretation of the location. These strategies replace a binding principle that has been lost, enabling the city to grow homogenously. Analogue to this approach, in the case of interventions of architectural scale, the auton-

Links/Left:
Museum der Bildenden Künste/
Museum of Fine Arts, Leipzig, 2004

Rechts/Right:
Erweiterung/Extension Kunsthalle
Bremen, 2011

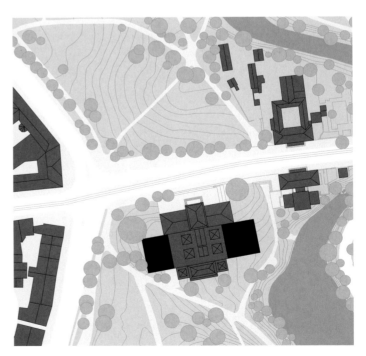

nischer Dimension die autonome Form des Gebäudes und dessen Verankerung am Ort ein dialektisches Gegensatzpaar. Eine Relation, die mit der Spannung zwischen Vorgabe und Gebäude, zwischen alten Strukturen und neuer Deutung des öffentlichen Raums arbeitet. Gegenläufige Vorgehensweisen bestimmen das Verhältnis von Architektur und Städtebau: Beim Leipziger Museumsquartier dehnt erst der entgegen der Wettbewerbsauslobung vorgeschlagene «Rückzug des Museums ins Blockinnere» die Wirksamkeit der Architektur in eine städtebauliche Dimension aus und erlaubt im Bezug auf die Leipziger Passagenkultur einen «Ort» für das neue Museum zu erschaffen. Im Gegensatz dazu begründet bei der Erweiterung der Kunsthalle Bremen die Wiederherstellung der räumlichen Kontinuität der die Stadt umschliessenden Wallanlagen eine Form der Architektur, die nicht, wie gewünscht, einseitig zum Bestand eine zeichenhafte Erweiterung anordnet, sondern gerade als typologische Transformation symmetrisch mit dem Bestand verbunden, eine der Lage im Landschaftsraum angemessene objekthafte Erscheinung ausbilden kann. Der Vorgehensweise, Architektur und Städtebau auf ihre gegensätzlichen Komponenten hin zu untersuchen, um ihre Grenzen in den Bereich des jeweils anderen zu erweitern, liegt die Erkenntnis zugrunde, dass wir uns heute primär in Bereichen unzulänglicher städtebaulicher und architektonischer Muster bewegen, die sich einer umfassenden planerischen Ordnung entziehen. Die Herausforderung unter diesen Prämissen ist – unabhängig davon, ob ein Ensemble eine eigene städtebauliche Figur ausbildet, ein Haus, einen städtischen Platz entstehen lässt oder Innenräume städtische Handlungsspielräume erschliessen –, innerhalb des zergliederten Gefüges der Stadt neue in sich geschlossene urbane Strukturen und kollektive Lebensräume zu schaffen. Eine Haltung, die weder vom Auseinanderfallen des Zusammenhangs zwischen Architektur und Städtebau als zwangsläufigem Ausdruck unserer Zeit ausgeht, noch die Rekonstruktion einer retrospektiven Stadtvorstellung zum Gegenstand hat, sondern von der Vorstellung geleitet ist, in einem fortwährenden dialektischen Diskurs Gegensätze der Stadt der Gegenwart zu verknüpfen.

Nicht vorgefasste architektonische Bilder oder ideale städtebauliche Modelle, die einer differenzierten Lebenswirklichkeit nicht gerecht werden, sondern generell alle Aspekte der gesellschaftlichen Realität mit den jeweils damit verbundenen Zwängen und Widersprüchen bilden das Potenzial, ein zeitgemässes Verhältnis von Architektur und Städtebau, von Objekt und Struktur zu entwickeln. Unabhängig davon, ob mit dem vorgeschlagenen Freilegen der Allerheiligen

omous shape of the building and the way it is rooted in the location creates a dialectic pair of opposites. This relationship works with the tension between the specifications and the building, between old structures and a new interpretation of the public space. Opposing approaches determine the relationship between architecture and urban development: In the case of the Leipzig museum quarter, it is the fact that the architecture expands to the scale of an urban development that makes an impact, rather than the "retreat of the museum into the interior of the block" as suggested by the call for submissions. This expansion enables a "location" to be created for the new museum, one that makes reference to the colonnades typical of Leipzig. In contrast to this, the extension of the Kunsthalle Bremen justifies, in reconstructing the spatial continuity of the city walls, a form of architecture that does not symbolically align itself on one side of the existing buildings as initially desired but instead succeeds in creating an object-like appearance that is appropriate to its location within the landscape in the form of a typological transformation that is symmetrically connected to the existing buildings. This method of exploring the opposing components of architecture and urban development in order to extend the limitations of the other respectively, is based on the realisation that today we are moving primarily within areas that show insufficient urban and architectural patterns and therefore cannot be subjected to an extensive planning structure. The

Zeichnung/Drawing: Yadegar Asisi, Berlin

Museum der Bildenden Künste, Leipzig
Museum of Fine Arts, Leipzig, 2004

Hofkirche in München die grossartige Vorstellung von Gottfried Semper aufgegriffen wird, am «Hinterhof» der Münchner Residenz den Marstallplatz als vierten umgebenden Stadtraum auszubilden oder die Versatzstücke divergierender Stadtmodelle, «sozialistische Hauptstadtplanung» und «Prachtstrasse Unter den Linden», sich in der neuen architektonischen Form des «Berliner Schlosses» verschränken – immer geht es im Wesentlichen darum, das vorhandene, problematische Material zu aktivieren und in neuen Zusammenhängen aufzuheben.

Der zurückgenommene Charakter und die «minimalistische», reduzierte Erscheinung der Architektur und der städtebaulichen Strukturen, die sich durch eine einfache Materialität sowie hohe räumliche Komplexität auszeichnen, sind in diesem Zusammenhang nicht selbstbezogenes «Kunstwollen», sondern erlauben in der formalen Beschränkung die Freiheit, beide Seiten eines mehrsinnigen Verhältnisses sichtbar zu machen, um Objekt und Struktur in eine neue, oft überraschende Beziehung zu setzen. Eine Beziehung zwischen Architektur und Stadt, die im besten Fall gleichzeitig radikal und beiläufig einfach ist: wenn beispielsweise beim solitär aufragenden, kristallinen Kubus des Leipziger Museums in den urbanen Innenräumen Architektur und Stadt zusammenfallen oder bei der Erweiterung der Kunsthalle Bremen das typologische Fortschreiben der objekthaften Erscheinung die stadträumliche Kontinuität der Wallanlagen wiederherstellt. Zur Anwendung kommt ein künstler-

Museum der Bildenden Künste, Leibzig
(Collage mit Randbebauung)
Museum of Fine Arts, Leibzig, 2004
(Collage with perimeter development)

challenge of this premise is – whether or not an ensemble takes on its own form in terms of urban planning and includes a house, an urban square or interior spaces that allow urbanistic scope of action – to create new self-contained urban structures and collective living spaces within the dismembered ensemble of the city. An approach that neither assumes the breakdown of the coherency between architecture and urban planning to be an inevitable expression of our time, nor focuses on the reconstruction of a retrospective concept of a city but is instead guided by the concept of connecting opposites within a contemporary city to create a continuous dialectic discourse.

Architectural images or ideal models of urban development that are not preconceived, which do not do justice to the differentiated reality of life with its associated constraints and contradictions, have the potential to create a contemporary relationship between architecture and urban development, between the object and the structure. Irrespective of whether or not the proposal to expose the Allerheiligen Hofkirche (All Saints' Court Chapel) in Munich takes up Gottfried Semper's wonderful vision to develop the Marstallplatz, in the "courtyard" of the Münchner Residenz (Munich Residency) as a fourth encompassing urban space or to take the incongruous divergent city models "socialist metropolis planning" and "grand boulevard Unter den Linden" and link them to the new architectural structure of the "Berliner Schloss" (Berlin City Palace) – the goal is always essentially to invoke the existing, problematic materials and enhance them through a new context.

The reserved nature and the "minimalist", reduced appearance of the architecture and urban structures, which are characterized by simple materials and a high level of spatial complexity, are not self-centred "Kunstwollen" (artistic ambition) in this context but in their formal limitations allow the freedom to make both sides of an ambiguous relationship visible, in order to put the object and structure in a frequently surprising relationship to one another. A relationship between architecture and the city, which at best is both radical and incidentally simple: for example when in the case of the solitaire, crystalline cube shape of the Leipzig Museum the urban architecture of the interior spaces and the city overlap or in the case of the extension of the Kunsthalle Bremen where the typological continuation of the object-like appearance restores the continuity of the city walls in terms of urban space. An artistic-analytical procedure is put into practice here, which relies neither on simple emulation nor grand scale – it takes two different directions, dividing and communicating at the same

isch-analytisches Verfahren, das weder auf einfache Nachahmung noch auf den grossen Stil setzt – es blickt in beide Richtungen, trennt und vermittelt zugleich. Das Eigenleben seiner gegensätzlichen Komponenten wird in einem Masse gesteigert, dass diese sich wie These und Antithese zueinander verhalten.

Wie immer man diese «Konfrontation», das ambivalente Verhältnis von Stadt und Architektur, von Objekt und Raum deutet, stets sind diese beiden Pole in einem Dialog begriffen, wobei jede Position abwechselnd Frage und Antwort enthält. Im Mittelpunkt steht die Vorstellung, im schöpferischen Weiterbauen neue urbane Zusammenhänge zu (er)finden, mit dem Ziel, Dauer und Veränderung, Vergangenheit und Zukunft jenseits unzeitgemässer Doktrin und ästhetischer Spekulation in eine permanente Kontinuität zu stellen.

time. The autonomous existence of its opposing components is enhanced to such a degree that these relate to one another like a thesis and antithesis. However one interprets this "confrontation", this ambivalent relationship between city and architecture, between object and space, these two poles are in constant dialogue with one another, whereby each position contains the question and answer respectively. The main focus is on the concept of discovering or inventing new urban contexts that put goals, duration and change, past and future, into a permanent state of continuity that is free of outmoded doctrines and aesthetic speculation.

Erweiterung Kunsthalle Bremen
Extension Kunsthalle Bremen, 2011

Thermalbad und Therapiezentrum, Bad Saarow

Hot Springs and Therapy Centre, Bad Saarow

Das neue Thermalbad steht in der Tradition von Gebäuden, die in Bad Saarow wie in anderen Kurorten einen speziellen Typus von öffentlichen Bauwerken mit Säulenhallen und Trinkbrunnen sowie neue Begegnungsräume wie Alleen und Wandelhallen hervorgebracht haben. Das raumgreifende Gebäudevolumen des Bads strukturiert, wie Bahnhof und historisches Kurhaus, die umgebende kleinteilige Villenstruktur Bad Saarows.

In Analogie zum denkmalgeschützten, von hölzernen dorischen Kolonnaden gefassten Bahnhof, als «repräsentativer Eingang zur Stadt», wird die raumgreifende U-förmige Anlage des Bades zum verbindenden Element zwischen Stadtpromenade und Landschaftsraum. Dies geschieht konkret mit der Ausbildung einer öffentlichen Durchwegung des Gebäudes; sowie architektonisch überdurch eine Säulenhalle als Eingang von der Kurpromenade her und durch hochaufragende schlanke Wandelgangpfeiler im Übergang zum kiefernbestandenen Park am See.

The new hot springs have been designed in a construction tradition that in Bad Saarow and other spa towns reflects a special type of public building with porticos and drinking fountains as well as new rooms for interaction, boulevards and galleries. The spacious building volumes of the hot springs structure the surrounding small-sectioned villa configuration found in Bad Saarow as it similarly does to the station and historical spa facility.

As an analogy to the listed station building encompassed by wooden, Doric colonnades, which forms a "representative entrance to the city", the spacious U-shaped facility of the spa forms a link between the town promenade and the surrounding landscape. This is also expressed specifically in the design of the public passageways running through the building as well as architecturally in the portico that forms the entrance to the spa promenade and in the high, slim colonnade pillars in the area of transition to the park at the lakeside containing pine trees.

Bauherrschaft/Client: Bad Saarow-Pieskow Kur- und Fremdenverkehrs GmbH, Bad Saarow
Projektwettbewerb/Project competition: 1995, 1. Preis/1st Prize (in zwei Phasen/in two phases)
Ausführung/Construction: Anfang 1996 – Ende 1998
Mitarbeiter/Collaboration: Susanne Dallmeyer, Anne Kirsch, Christian A. Müller
Bauleitung/Construction management: Büro am Lützowplatz, Berlin
Tragwerksplanung/Structural planning: Ingenieurbüro Albert Grage, Herford
Haustechnik/Installations: Ingenieurbüro Möller & Partner, Düsseldorf

Rechts/Right: Bahnhofsensemble Station ensemble. 1994.
Aus/From: Reinhard Kiesewetter, Bad Saarow-Pieskow – Am Märkischen Meer (Hrsg. Gemeinde Bad Saarow)

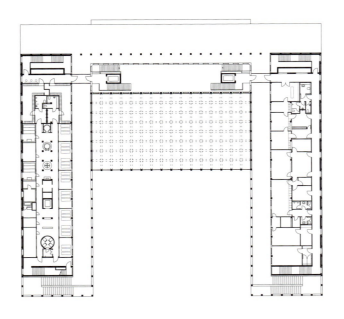

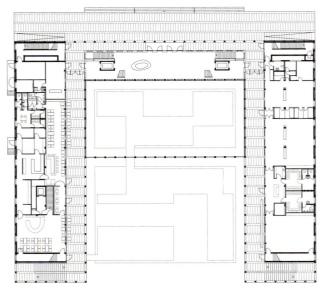
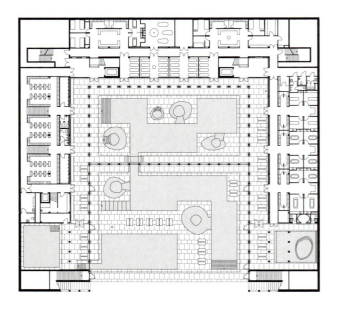

25 m

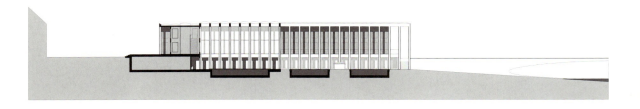

25 m

Studentenwohnheime, Brandenburg

Student Halls of Residence, Brandenburg

Das neue Baufeld der Studentenwohnheime im Vis-á-vis zu den blockhaften backsteinernen Kasernenbauten des Fachhochschulcampus bildet den Übergang von einer geschlossenen städtischen Bebauung in ein peripheres Umfeld. Der Ambivalenz des Ortes entsprechen horizontal ausgerichtete Einzelbaukörper, die sich – analog zu den Bauabschnitten – zu einer inselhaften Bauform zusammenfügen und den kommunikativen Charakter «studentischen Wohnens» zum Gegenstand haben. Der kommunikative Aspekt studentischen Wohnens wird dabei im besonderen Mass durch die kollektive Form sowie die Organisation der Gebäude um verbindende innere «Strassen und Plätze» bestimmt. Alle Wohnungen sind durch Flure und Laubengänge fussläufig verbunden. An den Schnittstellen der Wohnungstypologien sind grossmassstäbliche Lufträume, an die sich vertikale Erschliessungen und Gemeinschaftsbereiche lagern, ausgebildet. Die Lufträume im Wechsel mit differenzierten Wohnformen bilden sich direkt in der «Verräumlichung» der Fassaden ab.

The new construction site for the student halls of residence vis-á-vis the block-shaped brick barrack construction of the University of Applied Science campus forms the transition from a closed urban development to a peripheral environment. The ambivalence of the location corresponds to the horizontally aligned solitaires which – analogue to the construction stages – are combined to form an island-like structural shape and represent the communicative character of "student lifestyle". The communicative aspect of student life is characterised in particular by the collective nature as well as the organisation of the buildings around connecting "streets and squares" within the ensemble. All the apartments and can be reached by foot via corridors and arcades. There are large airspaces at the intersections between the different typologies of apartment, next to which vertical routes of access and common areas are located. The airspaces, which alternate with differentiated zones and styles of living are reflected directly in the "spatial expression" of the facades.

Bauherrschaft/Client: Studentenwerk Potsdam vertreten durch das Landesbauamt Brandenburg
Projektwettbewerb/Project competition: 1995, 1. Preis/1st Prize
Ausführung/Construction: Anfang 1996–Ende 1998
Mitarbeiter/Collaboration: Christian Müller (1. Bauabschnitt/1st construction phase); Inge Günther (2. Bauabschnitt/2nd construction phase)
Bauleitung/Construction management: WD Borchert, Berlin; Steffen Altenburg – einsbisneun, Berlin
Bauingenieur/Construction engineer: BAIG, Brandenburg (Tragwerksplanung/Structural planning); BWE, Ragow (Heizung, Lüftung, Sanitär/Heating, Ventilation, Sanitary)

Oben: Städtebauliche Ueberarbeitung
Top: Urban planning amendment
2003/2009

Unten: Städtebauliches Konzept
Bottom: Urban planning concept
Wettbewerb/Competition 1995

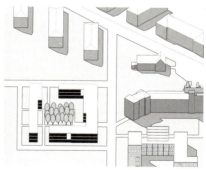

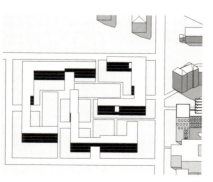

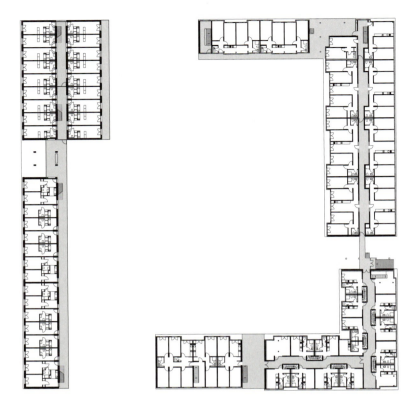

Unten: 2. Etappe; realisiert 2011
Below: 2nd construction phase; construction 2011

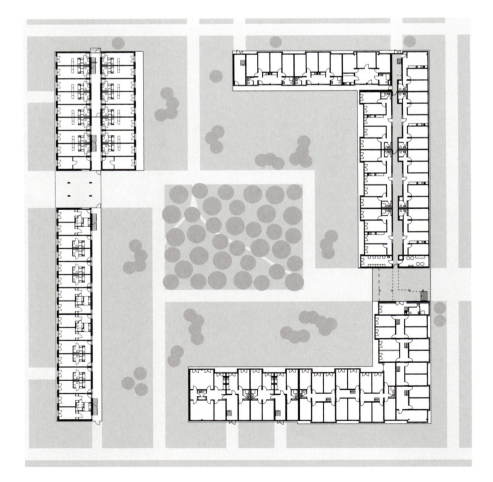

25 m

Museum der Bildenden Künste, Leipzig

Museum of Fine Arts, Leipzig

Das Potenzial des Entwurfs liegt in der Thematisierung des Widerspruchs, «Stadtreparatur» in einem kleinteiligen Umfeld mit einem repräsentativen, grossvolumigen Museumsbau zu leisten. Der die Häuser der Stadt überragende Museumsbau zieht sich in den Block zurück und wird umgeben von einem Ring kleinteiliger, städtischer Bebauung. Die extreme städtebauliche Form sucht ein Gleichgewicht zwischen autonomer Architektur und Verankerung am Ort. Die Autonomie der den skulpturalen Baukörper umfassenden gläsernen Hülle steht im Kontrast zur steinernen Stadt und thematisiert mit grossmassstäblichen, urbanen Innenräumen die für Leipzig spezifische Öffentlichkeit gläserner Passagen und Höfe. Die Verschränkung von Architektur und Stadt, von Innen- und Aussenraum hat das Ziel, den Charakter des Museums als neuen urbanen Ort Leipzigs darzustellen.

The potential of the design lies in the way it deals with the contradictory aspect of "repairing the city" with a representative, large-scale museum building in an environment made up of small sections. The building structure, which towers up above the other buildings in the city, retreats into the block and is surrounded by small, urban buildings. The extreme urban structure seeks a balance between autonomous architecture and the fact that it has its roots in the location. The autonomy of the glass envelope surrounding the sculptural building forms a contrast to the stony city, and with its large-scale, urban interior spaces it reflects the glass passages and courtyards that are typical of Leipzig's public spaces. The interaction between architecture and the city, between the interior and exterior space, has the goal of presenting the character of the museum as a new urban location in Leipzig.

Bauherrschaft/Client: Stadt Leipzig, Kulturamt
Projektwettbewerb/Project competition: 1997, 1. Preis/1st Prize (in zwei Phasen/in two phases)
Auszeichnung/Award: Kritikerpreis/Critic's prize 2005
Ausführung/Construction: 2004
Mitarbeiter/Collaboration: Anne Kirsch, Christian Müller, Jule Lienemeyer, Jürgen Reisch
Bauleitung/Construction management: Peter Flucke – einsbisneun, Berlin

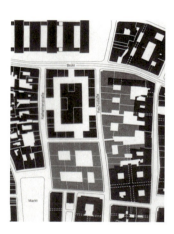

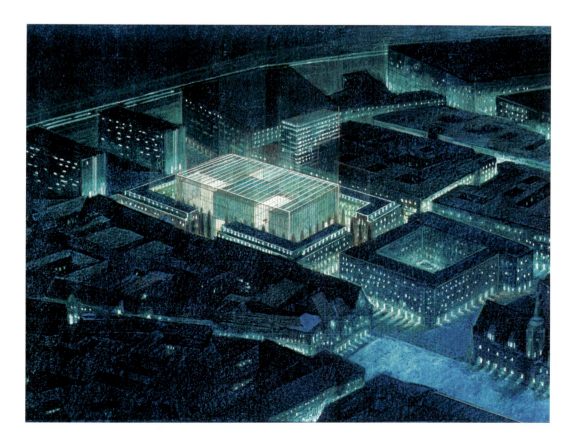

Mädler Passage, Leipzig

Zeichnung/Drawing: Yadegar Asisi, Berlin

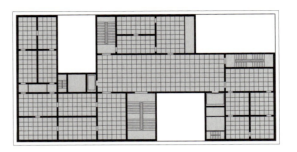

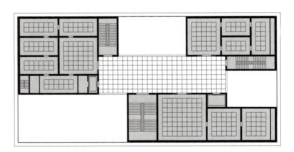

25 m

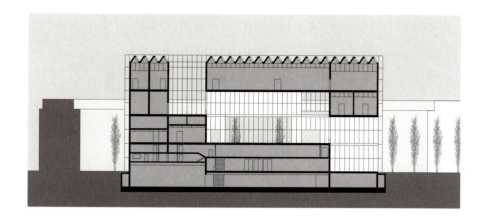
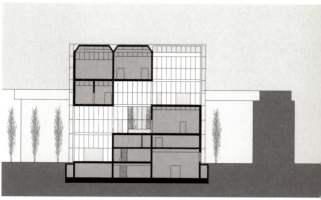

Sporthalle Max-Taut-Schule, Berlin

Sports Hall Max-Taut-School, Berlin

Die besonderen Herausforderungen bestanden darin, das aus der reformpädagogischen Bewegung der 20er Jahre entstandene denkmalgeschützte Schulprojekt Max Tauts im Massstab der Tautschen Aussenräume zu ergänzen und den südlich angrenzenden Erweiterungsbereich mit seinen objekthaften DDR-Plattenbauschulen stadt- und landschaftsplanerisch einzuordnen. Die kammartig zur geschwungenen Grossform der Schule und abweichend von der Wettbewerbsvorgabe an der Grundstücksgrenze situierte Halle folgt den Intentionen Tauts. Der aus Klinkersockel und Oberlichtband geschichtete neue Hallenbau nimmt Bezug auf die horizontal gegliederten Ziegelbauten der 20er Jahre, während sich der in Sichtbeton gegossene Umkleidetrakt als lineares Element mit der wiedererrichteten Gartenmauer und dem angrenzenden Landschaftsraum verbindet. Der externe Zugang zur Sporthalle entlang der Grundstücksgrenze ist öffentliche Durchwegung und architektonisches Rückgrat des Entwurfs.

The special challenge consisted of supplementing the listed school building project by Max Taut that emerged from the pedagogical reform movement in the 1920s to the same scale as the outdoor spaces designed by Taut and also to incorporate the area of extension bordering the site in the south with its object-like GDR "Plattenbau" or prefabricated school buildings in terms of town and landscape planning. The comb-shaped, undulating large school building structure and the location of the hall on the edge of the site that was not foreseen in the competition stipulations are in line with Taut's intention. The layered new hall building comprising of a clinker base and a strip of skylights makes reference to the horizontally structured brick buildings from the 1920s while the linear element of the changing room tract in exposed concrete links the reconstructed garden wall to the adjacent landscape area. The external access to the sports hall along the site boundary comprises the public thoroughfares and the architectural spine of the design proposal.

Bauherrschaft/Client: Senatsverwaltung für Stadtentwicklung Berlin
Wettbewerb: 1. Preis (im beschränkten Gutachterverfahren)/Competition: 1st Prize
Ausführung/Construction: 2004
Mitarbeit/Collaboration: Jürgen Reisch
Bauleitung/Construction management: Döpping Widell, Berlin
Tragwerksplanung/Structural planning: Professor Dr. Ing. Hilbers, Berlin
Haustechnik/Installations: Ingenieurbüro Schwidurski, Grünheide
Elektrotechnik/Electrical engineering: Schmidt Olufsen, Berlin
Landschaftsarchitekten/Landscape architects: Lützow 7, Berlin

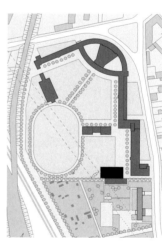

Schulanlage/School facility: Max Taut

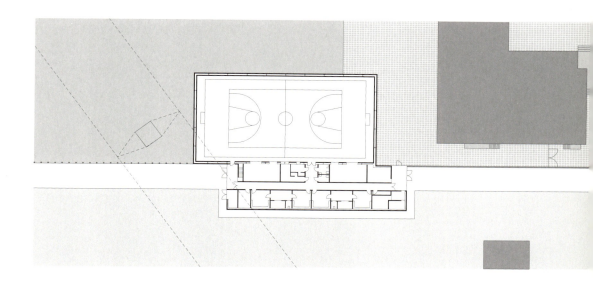

Erweiterung Kunsthalle Bremen

Extension Kunsthalle Bremen

Der Entwurf zur Erweiterung der Kunsthalle Bremen geht von zwei wesentlichen Gedanken aus: einem typologischen Ansatz zur Transformation des Bestandes in eine neue ganzheitliche Bauform und von einer Wiederherstellung der verloren gegangenen landschaftsräumlichen Kontinuität der begrünten Wallanlagen.

Abweichend von der Wettbewerbsvorgabe, das Bauvolumen einseitig anzuordnen, wird die Baumasse in zur Achse des Kernbaus von 1849 und 1899 annähernd symmetrische Kuben geteilt. Diese gleichgewichtige Setzung der Baukörper betont die Autonomie der Kunsthalle im Landschaftsraum und stellt die räumliche Kontinuität der Wallanlagen wieder her. Alt- und Neubau bilden eine kreuzförmige bauliche Struktur. Die Neue Kunsthalle Bremen – ihre äussere Erscheinung, ihr innerer Aufbau – ist als einheitliches Ganzes wahrnehmbar gefügt aus älteren und neueren historischen Schichten.

The design proposal for the extension of the Kunsthalle Bremen is based on two principal ideas: a typological approach to the transformation of the existing buildings in the form of a new holistic construction and a reconstruction of the lost continuity of the landscape represented by the city wall covered with greenery.

Although the competition requirements specified that the building volume be aligned to one side, the construction volume will be divided up in almost symmetrical cubes along the axis of the core building built between 1849 and 1899. This equally weighted alignment of the building structures emphasizes the au- tonomy of the Kunsthalle within the landscape and reconstructs the spatial continuity of the city wall. Old and new buildings form a cross-shaped building structure. The Neue Kunsthalle Bremen – both its exterior appearance and the interior design – has been visibly created from older and more recent historical layers to form a unified whole.

Bauherrschaft/Client: Kunstverein Bremen
Wettbewerb/Competition: 2005, 1. Preis/1st Prize
Ausführung/Construction: 2011
Planung/Planning: Nadine Clauss, Michael Eisele, Jasmin Scheckenbach
Bauleitung/Construction management: Stephanie Allmers, Jan Bremermann, Michael Eisele, Florian Fels, Anja Gentner, Jasmin Scheckenbach

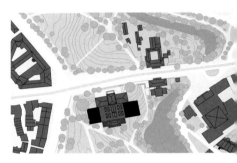

Aus/From: Den Bildenden Künsten geweiht – 150 Jahre Kunsthalle. Delmenhorst: Verlag Aschenbeck & Holstein

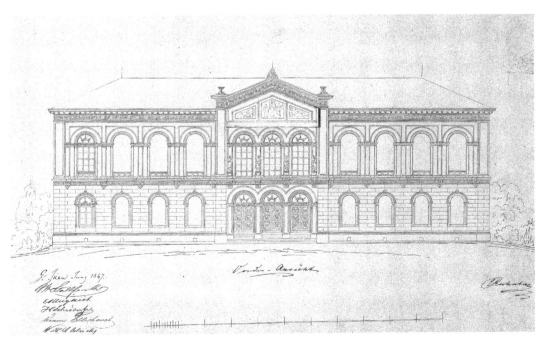

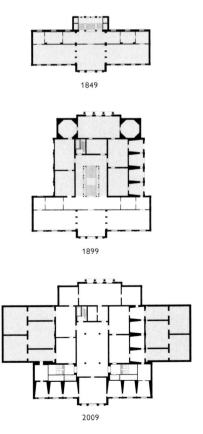

1849

1899

2009

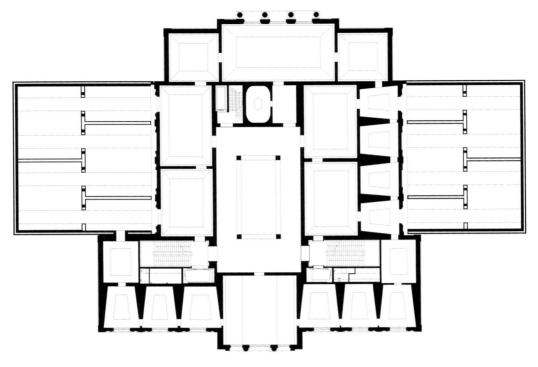

1. Obergeschoss – Ausstellungsebene II/1st floor - Exhibition level II

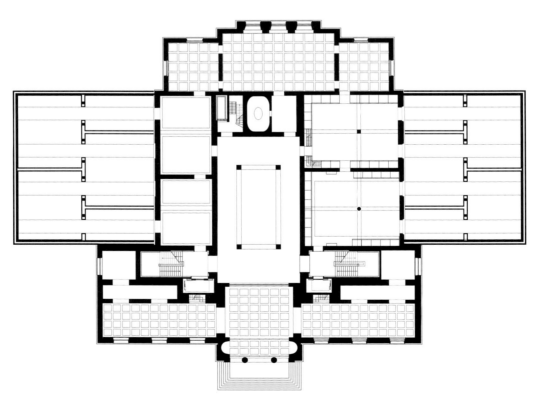

Eingangsgeschoss – Ausstellungsebene I/Ground floor - Exhibition level I

20 m

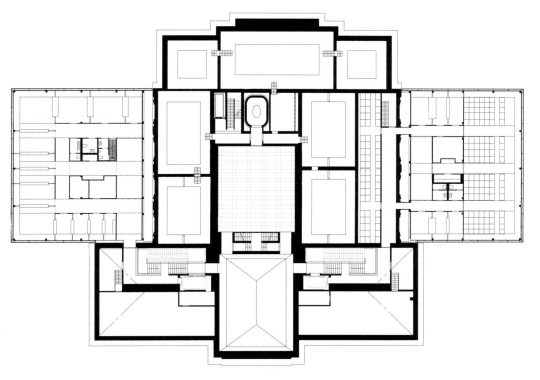

2. Obergeschoss – Verwaltungsebene/2nd floor – Administration level

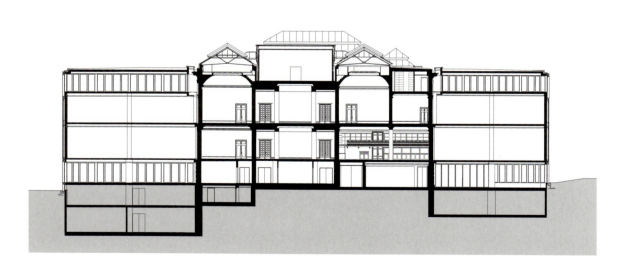

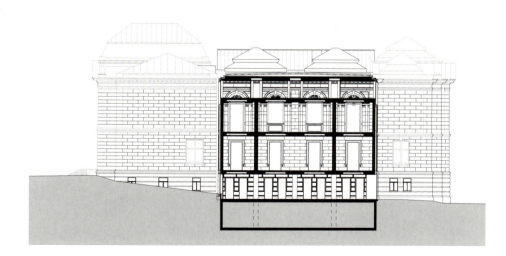

20 m

Der Marstallplatz als Komplettierung der Münchner Residenz

The Marstallplatz as the Completion of a Residence in Munich

Wettbewerbsentwurf/Competition design: Hufnagel Pütz Rafaelian

Städtebauliche Planung von Gottfried Semper 1866/67. Aus/From: Martin Fröhlich, Gottfried Semper. Zürich: Verlag für Architektur 1991 (studiopaperback)

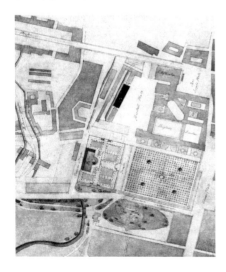

Städtebau

Ausgangspunkt unserer Arbeit ist die Interpretation des Ortes als eine Sequenz von Stadträumen. Raumschichten, die stadtmorphologisch und historisch latent vorhanden sind, werden neu gelesen und herausgearbeitet. Wir greifen die Idee Leo von Klenzes, am Marstall eine Piazza zur östlichen Komplettierung der Residenz zu schaffen, in neuer Form wieder auf. Durch den Gedanken, die Residenz mit vier typischen Stadträumen zu umgeben, dem Max-Joseph-Platz, dem Odeonsplatz, dem Hofgarten und dem Marstallplatz, bildet sich ein ausserordentlicher stadträumlicher Abschluss der Residenz nach Osten.

Der Marstall verweist nicht nur durch seine aus der Richtung der Residenz herausgedrehte Lage, sondern auch durch seine historische Funktion und seinen Charakter als Zweckbau auf die besondere hierarchische Ordnung zu den Repräsentationsbauten der Residenz. Eine den Grünraum begleitende «Zeilenbebauung» an der Marstallstrasse macht die Orientierung der Reithalle von Klenzes auf die Residenz wieder nachvollziehbar, ermöglicht also dessen städtebauliche Einbindung und vermeidet eine Konkurrenz zweier Freiflächen westlich bzw. östlich der Reithalle. Die Bebauung entlang der Marstallstrasse definiert den Übergang zum östlich anschliessenden Stadtkörper und bildet mit seinen angeschnittenen Zeilenköpfen einen ruhigen Rhythmus zum Karl-Scharnagel-Ring der zur strassenbegleitenden Randbebauung des Stadtrings überleitet.

Wesentlich für die Qualität des neuen Platzraumes ist der Gedanke das nach den Zerstörungen des 2. Weltkriegs gänzlich ahistorisch situierte, die Allerheiligenhofkirche verriegelnde Kulissenmagazingebäude des Nationaltheater zu entfernen. Die Stellung des Gebäudes vor der Hauptfassade der Allerheiligenhofkirche beraubt ein sakrales Schlüsselwerk Klenzes seiner städtebaulichen Wirkung. Die Option, das Kulissenmagazin zu verlagern, lässt eine grossartige Raumidee heute in greifbare Nähe rücken: von Klenzes Vorstellung der Platzarchitektur von San Marco, die Allerheiligenhofkirche – eine Nachbildung der Capella Palatina in Palermo – im Gegenüber zur Reithalle als Zentrum der Platzanlage. Der Ort wird aus seiner Randlage befreit zu einem gleichwertigen und räumlich eigenständigen Element aufgewertet.

Architektur

Die den neuen Platzraum bildende kompakte Bebauung für die Zentrale der Max-Plank-Gesellschaft ist ein konventionelles zweibündiges Verwaltungsgebäude mit aussenliegenden Büroeinheiten und einer grosszügigen inneren Strasse. Der Rand wird durchstossen von grossmassstäblichen transparenten

Town Planning

The starting point for our work is the interpretation of the location as a sequence of urban spaces. Layers of space that are existent in an urban-morphological and historically latent sense are re-interpreted and developed. We have taken up the idea expounded by Leo von Klenzes to complete the residence in a new way in the form of a piazza in the area of the Marstall. The idea of surrounding the residence with four typical urban spaces, the Max-Joseph-Platz, the Odeonsplatz, the Hofgarten and the Marstallplatz creates a unique urban completion to the east-facing residence.

The Marstall square not only indicates its special hierarchical alignment towards the representative residence buildings by means of its historical function and its purpose-built character. The "terraced housing" along the Marstallstrasse that supplements the green area makes the fact that the riding arena designed by Klenzes faces towards the residency plausible once again and thus enables it to be incorporated into the urban environment and prevents the two open spaces west and east of the riding arena from competing with one another. The building along the Marstallstrasse defines the transition to the urban structure in the east and with the truncated buildings at the end of the row creates a calm rhythmic transition to the Karl-Scharnagel-Ring which in turn leads to the peripheral development along the ring road around the city.

An important qualitative feature of the new square or open space is the idea of removing the warehouse storing the stage scenery of the national theatre, which is, following the destruction caused by the Second World War, in no way historically situated and blocks the Allerheiligenhofkirche. Its position in front of the main façade of this building robs a key sacral work by Klenz of its urban impact. The option of moving the stage scenery storage building now puts a great spatial concept within reach: Klenzes' idea of the architecture set in the square of San Marco and the Allerheiligenhofkirche – a replica of the Capella Palatina in Palermo – as a counterpart to the riding arena that forms the centre of the site. The location is thus freed of its fringe status and enhanced, making it an equal and spatially autonomous element.

Architecture

The compact building development that forms the site of the square on which the Max-Plank-Society headquarters are to be built is a conventional, two-volume, double-loaded administration building with exterior office units and a spacious street on the interior. Large transparent volumes cut through the

Volumen, Raumeinschübe, die sich aus dem Verhältnis zum Aussenraum und zur inneren Funktion entwickeln. Sie vermitteln als Teil der Platz- bzw. Grünfassade zwischen kleinteiligen Bürogeschossen und dem Massstab von Residenz und Marstall und ermöglichen gleichzeitig das Unterbringen von auf die Bürostruktur bezogenen grossmassstäblichen Sonderfunktionen. Diese durchbrechen die Geschossigkeit der Bürostruktur, sind interne vertikale Verbindungselemente zwischen den Abteilungen und belichten als grosse, transparente Öffnungen die inneren Strassen und Binnenhallen. Strassen und Binnenhallen formulieren kommunikative, gemeinschaftliche Flächen des Gebäudes. In den jeweiligen Umkehrungen der Raumeinschübe, als gläserne Kuben zum Grünraum und als grüne Wintergärten zum Platz, wird die Ambivalenz des Gebäudes, Filter zwischen und Teil unterschiedlicher Stadträume und Qualitäten zu sein, spürbar. Die bauliche Struktur ist komplett aus Sichtbeton gegossen, der durch Zuschläge der Farbigkeit von Residenz und Marstall angenähert wird. Alle zwei Geschosse auskragende Deckenplatten tragen die vorgehängten Fassaden: Zum städtischen Platz und zur Residenz eine rahmenlose Structural Glazing Fassade, zu Grünraum und Hofgarten das hölzerne Rankgerüst der «Orangeriefassaden». Die unterschiedlichen Aussenräume werden in den Fassaden thematisiert. Der steinerne Platz wird zur gläsernen Stadtfassade, der Grünraum zur begrünten Raumhülle. Die Autonomie der Raumhüllen bildet den Rahmen, profane Nutzung und stadträumliche Bedeutung des Ortes in Einklang zu bringen.

edge of the street – insertions into the space that are created from the relationship between the outside space and the inner function. They mediate, as part of the façade of the square and the green area, between the small scale of the office storeys and the dimensions of the Residenz and the Marstall and are able to accommodate the large special functions that are based on the office structure. These penetrate the structural levels of the office building and form internal vertical connecting elements between the departments, illuminating the interior streets and halls by means of the large, transparent openings. The latter convey the communicative, communal nature and zones of the building. In the respective inversions created by these insertions into the space, in the form of glass cubes overlooking the green area or green conservatories overlooking the square, the ambivalence of the building that acts as a filter between the different urban spaces and qualities while at the same time being part of them, becomes tangible. The structure of the building has been cast completely in exposed concrete, which has been supplemented by colour in order to create more similarity to the Residenz and the Marstall. Both storeys with protruding ceiling panels serve as supports for the curtain-type facades: facing onto the urban square is a frameless structural glazing facade, while the wooden trellis of the "orangery façades" overlooks the green area and the courtyard garden. The different exterior areas will be reflected in the facades. The stony square becomes a glass urban façade, the green area a spatial envelope covered with greenery. The autonomous nature of the spatial envelope creates the framework for bringing the profane utilization and the urban importance of the location in tune with one another.

Modell Wettbewerb/Model competition

Städtebauliche Situation zur Residenz/ Residence urban planning site

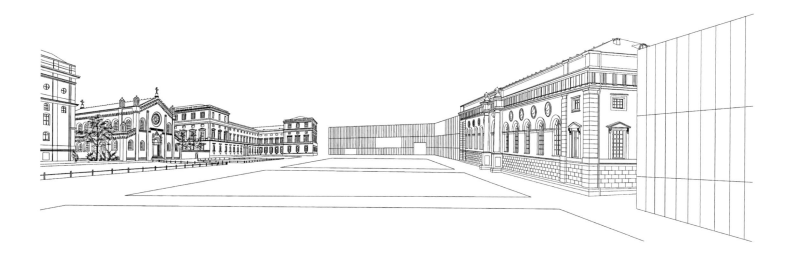

Erweiterung der Museumsinsel, Berlin

Extension of Museumsinsel, Berlin

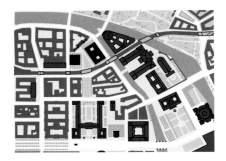

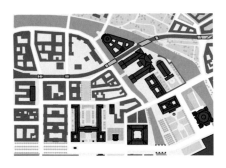

Oben/Top: Städtebauliches Konzept
Urban planning concept
Wettbewerb/Competition 2007

Mitte/Middle:
Bestand/Existing structure

Planung/Planning: Alfred Messel
1907–1909
Aus/From: Hans Reuther, Die
Museumsinsel in Berlin. Berlin:
Propyläen Verlag

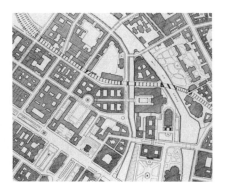

Städtebau

Die Museumsinsel ist einer der Orte, die als Teil des kollektiven Gedächtnisses auf besondere Weise mit der Geschichte und dem Selbstverständnis Berlins verbunden sind. Beginnend mit dem Bau des Alten Museums von Schinkel wuchs hier in hundert Jahren von 1830 bis 1930 ein einzigartiges kulturelles Erbe. Das Faszinierende, das Insulare ihrer Lage, ist die gleichzeitige Isolation und räumliche Begrenzung. Wenn nach der umfassenden Sanierung, der Wiederherstellung des Neuen Museums und Umwidmung der Depots und Keller zur Archäologischen Promenade die Reserven ausgeschöpft sind, wird das Begrenzte der Museumsinsel und die Notwendigkeit, den historischen Kulturstandort nicht nur zu sichern, sondern weiterzuentwickeln, zur dringlichen Aufgabe. Vorausschauend fällt der Blick dabei auf zwei Orte, den Schlossplatz und das Gelände der ehemaligen Kasernen im Gegenüber zum Bode-Museum. Während die Nutzung des Schlossplatzes die Museumsnutzungen gleichsam auf ihren Ursprung zurückführen würde, markiert die Ausweitung über den Kupfergraben hinweg einen Traditionsbruch. Die Enge der Insel wird verlassen, die Verbindung des Kulturkomplexes mit den umliegenden Stadtbezirken eingegangen. Diese Erweiterung kann nur unter Wahrung des einzigartigen Charakters der Berliner Museumsinsel erfolgen. So wie auf dem Gelände des Packhofs die «deutsche Akropolis der Kunst» auf der Spreeinsel als utopischer Traum hervorgegangen ist, bedarf deren Fortschreibung auf dem Kasernenareal einer zeitgemässen Interpretation dessen, was Kultur heute sein will.

Den Monumenten der Museumsinsel wird mit dem urbanen Ensemble der Museumshöfe, mit der Suche nach einem Bindeglied zwischen städtischer Textur und von Objekten bestimmtem städtischem Raum, geantwortet. Eine spezifische bauliche Form, lesbar in der Tradition der grossen Solitäre, wie auch als Teil der Blockstadt Berlins. Eine Intervention blockbildender Solitäre erlaubt sowohl eine signifikante Erscheinung, als auch die Einbindung in die Stadtstruktur, oder einfacher: sie thematisiert die Öffnung der Insel zur Stadt unter Wahrung ihrer Identität. Ein Gedanke, den schon Ludwig Hoffmann 1912 mit seinem Plan, die Museumsinsel als «Freistätte für Kunst und Wissenschaft» mit dem Humboldt-Forum zu verbinden, formuliert hat. Der Wettbewerbsbeitrag sucht nicht nur den hermetischen Charakter des Kasernenareals aufzubrechen, sondern begreift die dadurch möglich werdende Aktualisierung einer Bildungsidee als Chance, diese aus der isolierten Lage eines Kunsttempels in die angrenzenden Stadträume und zu neuen Inhalten zu führen.

Urban planning

The Museumsinsel (Museum Island) is one of the places that has a special connection to the history and self-perception of Berlin as part of collective memory. Beginning with the construction of the Alte Museum by Schinkel, a unique cultural heritage developed here in the hundred years between 1830 and 1930. The fascinating, insular aspect of this location at the same time means isolation and spatial limitation. If following the extensive renovation, the restoration of the Neue Museum and the reallocation of the storage rooms and cellar the reserves have been used up, the limitations of the Museumsinsel and the need to not only secure the historical cultural centre but also to further develop it, has become an urgent task. Looking ahead, the attention turns to two locations, the Schlossplatz and the site of the former barracks opposite the Bode-Museum. While the utilization of the Schlossplatz would at the same time mean a return to the original utilization of the museums, the extension out beyond the Kupfergraben represents a break with tradition. The limitations of the island have been departed from and a connection has been made between the cultural complex and the surrounding city quarters. This extension can only take place if the unique character of the Berlin Museumsinsel is maintained. Just as on the site of the Packhof the "German acropolis of art" has emerged on the Spreeinsel as a utopian dream, the continuation of it on the site of the barracks demands a contemporary interpretation of what culture seeks to be today.

The urban ensemble of the museum courtyards with their search for a link between urban texture and urban space determined by objects are a response to the monumental aspect of the Museumsinsel – a specific form of construction that can be read in the tradition of large solitary buildings, as well as part of the block city of Berlin. An intervention with buildings that together form a block creates a significant appearance as well as incorporating the island into the city structure, or put more simply: it refers to the opening up of the island while still maintaining its identity. An idea that Ludwig Hoffmann expressed back in 1912 with his plan to link the Museumsinsel as a "sanctuary for art and science" with the Humboldt-Forum. The competition contribution not only seeks the hermetic character of the barracks site but also conceives that the updating of an educational concept be made possible here as a chance of leading these from their isolated position as a temple of art out to the surrounding urban spaces and to new content. Buildings that have been positioned independently of one another and new green areas link

Voneinander unabhängig gesetzte Baukörper und neue Grünräume vernetzen die Museumshöfe mit dem Stadtorganismus. Eine Bewegungslinie verbindet entlang der Hochbahn, ausgehend vom Bode-Museum, über die Museumshöfe, die neue zentrale Universitätsbibliothek bis hin zum Bahnhof Friedrichstrasse, kollektive Orte urbaner Dimension.

Architektur
Ohne dies im Rahmen der städtebaulichen Aufgabe auszuformulieren, intendiert die zugrunde liegende Konzeption ein präzises architektonisches Bild. Die straffe Ausbildung der Kubatur und die materielle steinerne Präsenz vermitteln Modernität und Dauerhaftigkeit. Der volumetrische Auftritt der Neubauten im Stadtbild, die Ausbildung der Grünräume, selbstbewusst und eigenständig, aber eingebunden in ein neues Ganzes, scheinen angemessen, die Tradition der Staatlichen Museen Berlins weiterzutragen. Die Architektur folgt der Geschichte des Ortes und spiegelt den geistigen Anspruch der Aufgabe.

Die Einfachheit, fast Beiläufigkeit des Konzeptes gewährleistet bei nicht im Detail voraussehbaren Entwicklungsszenarien in jeder Phase eine nachhaltige Verbesserung der Stadtgestalt. Grundkonzeption und kompakte Bauvolumen machen eine Errichtung in Baustufen möglich. Bereits in der ersten Phase formulieren die angedachten Baufelder städtische Räume, Plätze und Strassen und lassen diese schrittweise fortschreiben.

Die Baukörper sind in ihrer Nutzung weitgehend offen, wobei ihre Lage und Typologie Hinweise zu den Nutzungsschwerpunkten geben. Während der in Dreiecksform um einen Hof ergänzte Kasernenblock die von der Museumsinsel verlagerten Funktionen von Werkstätten und technischen Diensten aufnehmen könnte, erhöht sich der Grad von Öffentlichkeit bei dem die Blockhöhen moderat überragenden, objekthaften westlichen Bauteil. Im Bezug zum neuen Medienzentrum der Universität und zum Humboldt-Forum lassen Besucherdienste, Forschungseinrichtungen und Archive Synergieeffekte erwarten. Das dritte solitäre Objekt am Wasser, prominent am Kupfergraben im Vis-à-vis zum Bode-Museum und in der Dimension darauf bezogen, ist prädestiniert, einen ersten grossen Schritt für eine bauliche Erweiterung der Staatlichen Museen zu Berlin, also ein neues Museum, zu denken.

the museum courtyards to the city organism. A line of movement forms a connection between collective locations with urban dimensions, running along the route of the elevated railway, beginning at the Bode-Museum, across the museum courtyards and the new central university library, to the station Friedrichstrasse.

Architecture
Without going into detail in terms of the urban planning task, the concept here tends towards the creation of a precise architectural image. The tight design of the cubature and the stony presence of the materials communicate modernism and consistency. The volumetric appearance of the new buildings in the urban cityscape, the design of the green areas that is self-assured and autonomous but incorporated into a new whole, seem to be appropriate for continuing the tradition of the Staatlichen Museen Berlin (Berlin State Museums). The architecture follows the history of the location and reflects the intellectual demands of the task.

The simplicity, the almost random nature of the concept, guarantees a sustainable enhancement to the cityscape during each phase in the case of unpredictable development scenarios. A basic concept and compact volumes make it possible to construct the building in phases. In the first phase the conceived building plots already express urban spaces, squares and streets and allow them to be developed step by step.

The future utilisation of the buildings has been left open to a large extent, although their location and typology do give an indication of their key utilisation aspects. While the triangular block of barracks arround a courtyard is able to accommodate the functions of the workshops and technical services that have been moved from the Museumsinsel, the public nature of the object-like building element in the west, which extends moderately above the height of the blocks, is increased. In relation to the new media centre of the university and the Humboldt-Forum, visitor services, research institutes and archive synergy effects are anticipated. The third solitary object by the water, set in a prominent position in the Kupfergraben opposite the Bode-Museum, using its scale as a point of reference, is predestined to conceive the first major step in a constructional extension to the Staatlichen Museen zu Berlin, in other words a new museum.

Humboldt Universität «Stadtschloss», Berlin

Humboldt-Forum City Palace (Stadtschloss), Berlin

Wettbewerbsentwurf/Competition design: Hufnagel Pütz Rafaelian

Stadtschloss vor dem 2. Weltkrieg/ Stadtschloss before World War II. Aus/From: Helmut Engel, Schauplatz Mitte. Berlin: Jovis Verlag 1998

Leitidee
Der Vorschlag für das neue Humboldt-Forum geht von der Überzeugung aus, dass die Suche nach der «verlorenen Mitte Berlins» der Einsicht bedarf, die am Ort vorgefundenen Strukturen als Ausdruck unterschiedlicher zeithistorischer und gesellschaftlicher Modelle zum Gegenstand der Betrachtung zu nehmen. Dabei können vorurteilsfrei gesehen gerade die vermeintlich antithetischen, ihrer Mitten beraubten Gegensatzpaare – im Westen die Allee Unter den Linden mit dem verlorenen Stadtschloss als räumlichen und ideellen Bezugspunkt und im Osten der abgerissene Palast der Republik, gedacht als bauliche und gesellschaftliche Einheit mit Marx-Engels-Forum und Fernsehturm – das Potential eines neuen identitätsstiftenden Zentrums für die Gesamtstadt bilden. In der ambivalenten städtebaulichen Figur, dem umschlossenen Eingangshof, der den Stadtraum nach Westen besetzt, und dem offenen Wasserhof, der als «Cour d´honneur» nach Osten einen Raum an der Spree ausbildet, verschränken sich die Gegensatzpaare. Die Rudimente der stadträumlichen Strukturen werden als «Materialien» des Genius Loci erfahrbar gemacht und werden auf unterschiedlichen Bedeutungsebenen zur integrativen Leitidee für die Rückgewinnung der Mitte der Stadt. Im Humboldt-Forum verbinden sich damit nicht nur in baulich konzeptioneller Weise die angrenzenden stadträumlichen Qualitäten, sondern es wird der Versuch unternommen, Geschichte auszusöhnen, aufgebrochene Gegensätze aufzuheben und im Neuen zu überwinden. Welche inhaltliche Nutzung wäre dazu besser geeignet als die Vision des neuen Humboldt-Forums, eine Bildungsutopie, die bei allen Widersprüchen und historischen Brüchen ihre Bezugspunkte im Motto Friedrich Wilhelm IV «Die Museumsinsel als Freistätte für Kunst und Wissenschaft» ebenso finden kann wie im sozialutopischen «Volkshausgedanken» oder im Humanismus der Brüder Wilhelm und Alexander von Humboldt.

Architektur und Städtebau
Stadträumlich formuliert das konzentrierte Volumen des Humboldt-Forums in der Kubatur des Stadtschlosses den baulichen und symbolischen Abschluss der Strasse Unter den Linden, während sich die Gegenseite über die Spree hinweg mit einer grosszügigen raumgreifenden Geste zum Grünraum des Marx-Engels-Forums und zum Fernsehturm öffnet. Der Lindenallee als Flaniermeile Berlins wird die landschaftliche Weite eines grünen Parks im Zentrum der Stadt gegenübergestellt. Bei der Annäherung von der Schlossfreiheit und im Übergang zum Eingangshof des Humboldt-Forums ist die Stülersche Kuppel

Guiding Principles
The proposal for the new Humboldt-Forum is based on the conviction that the search for the "lost centre of Berlin" should consider the structures found on location as an expression of different historical and social models. In doing so particularly the supposedly antithetic pairs of opposites that have been robbed of their centres are shown impartially – in the west the avenue Unter den Linden with the Stadtschloss (Berlin City Palace) that has been lost as an ideal point of reference and in the east the demolished Palast der Republik, intended to form a social unit with the Marx-Engels-Forum and the television tower – and encompass the potential of a new identity-forming centre for the city as a whole. In the ambivalent urban development scheme, the enclosed entrance courtyard, which occupies the urban space towards the west, and the open water courtyard, which as a "Cour d´honneur" forms a space in the east by the river Spree, the pairs of opposites interlink. The rudimentary building structure of the urban space are made experiencable as "materials" of the Genius Loci and become the integrative guiding principle behind the reclamation of the city centre. In the Humboldt-Forum the adjacent urban spatial qualities are not only combined in a structurally conceptual manner but an attempt is also made to reconcile history, to balance out broken opposites and overcome them by means of something new. What contextual utilisation could be more suited to this than the vision of the new Humboldt-Forum, an educational utopia that finds its point of reference, despite all its contradictions and historical fractures, in the motto of Friedrich Wilhelm IV: "the Museumsinsel as a sanctuary for art and science" just as much as in the social-utopian "Volkshaus" (people's house) concept or in the humanism of the brothers Wilhelm and Alexander von Humboldt.

Architecture and Urban Planning
In terms of urban planning the concentrated volumes of the Humboldt-Forum in the cubature of Stadtschloss represents the structural and symbolic completion of the street Unter den Linden, while the other side overlooking the River Spree opens out towards the green areas of the Marx-Engel Forum and the television tower with a generous, space-filling gesture. The Lindenallee, Berlin's promenade, forms a counterpart to the scenic expanse of a green park in the centre of the city. When coming closer to the Schlossfreiheit and in the transition to the entrance courtyard of the Humboldt-Forum, the cupola designed by Stüler above the Eosander portal is the determining architectural motif. On the side where

über dem Eosanderportal das bestimmende architektonische Motiv. Spreeseitig antwortet, in Analogie zu den Kolonnaden der Museumsinsel, ein öffentlicher Wandelgang, der einen abgesenkten «Wasserhof» umschliesst. Im Innern bilden der Hof als urbaner Festraum und die Wandelgänge zum Wasser kollektive Räume mit hoher Aufenthaltsqualität für die Menschen der Stadt. Diese gegensätzlichen Bilder können nicht nur als isolierte Architekturmotive verstanden werden, sondern tragen etwas von zwei Stadt- oder Denkmodellen in sich: Die Kuppel als Dominante im Stadtraum, als politisch und geistiger Mittelpunkt, ruht in sich selbst, ist auf festes Land gegründet, während die Kolonnaden als Element der Bewegung antithetisch auf das unsichere, in die Ferne ziehende Element des Wassers verweisen. Nähe und Ferne, Selbstvergewisserung und Verheissung werden zum architektonischen Bild für einen lebendigen Ort des Austausches, der neben den Sammlungen der aussereuropäischen Kunst und Kulturen und renommierten Wissenschaftssammlungen die Forschungseinrichtungen der Humboldt-Universität und die Zentral- und Landesbibliothek Berlin aufnehmen soll.

Die Architektur der «Neuen Mitte» der Gesamtstadt kann sich unter den beschriebenen Prämissen nicht in der Restauration und Rekonstruktion des «Verschwundenen» erschöpfen, sondern muss, will sie integrative Kraft entfalten, den unterschiedlichen Bedeutungsebenen in der architektonischen Erscheinung baulichen Ausdruck verleihen. Die neu gefundene Kubatur des Humboldtforums spiegelt in abstrakter Form Struktur und Massstäblichkeit des Stadtschlosses. Nur die in das Gesamtvolumen eingefügten «Schlossportale» werden als herausgehobene Zugänge in ihrer inneren und äusseren Form bis in die Details des Fassadenschmucks und der prächtigen barocken Innenarchitektur historisch getreu rekonstruiert. Ziel ist es, in der klaren Ablesbarkeit neuer und rekonstruierter Bereiche die Bedeutung des Stadtschlosses als einen wichtigen, aber nicht ausschliesslichen Teil der Geschichte des Ortes, im neuen Humboldt-Forum kenntlich zu machen.

the River Spree is located, a public colonnade that encloses a sunken "water courtyard" responds, in analogy to the colonnades on the Museumsinsel. In the interior, the courtyard as an urban space for festivities and the colonnades leading down to the water form qualitative collective spaces for the city residents. These contradictory images can not only be perceived as isolated architectural motifs but also contain two urban planning models or schools of thought: The dome as a dominant feature in the cityscape, as a political and spiritual centre, is calm and focused, founded on solid ground, while the colonnades as an element of movement antithetically make reference to the unstable element of water that draws one into the distance. Closeness and distance, self-assurance and promise become the architectural vision for a lively place of exchange that – in addition to the collections of non-European art and culture and the renowned scientific collections – is to accommodate the research facilities of the Humboldt University and the Zentral- und Landesbibliothek Berlin (The Central and Regional Library Berlin).

In view of the premises described, the architecture of the "new centre" of the city as a whole should not exhaust itself in the restoration and reconstruction of what has "disappeared" but must, and seeks to develop integrative strength, to lend structural expression to the different levels of meaning in the architectural appearance. The newly-discovered cubature of the Humboldt Forum reflects the structure and scale of the Stadtschloss in an abstract way. Only the "palace portals" inserted into the overall volume will be reconstructed so that they are identical to their predecessors – in the form of entrances that are singled out in their inner and outer form, right down to the detail of the façade ornamentation and the magnificent baroque interior design. The goal is to make the importance of the Stadtschloss as a significant yet not exclusive part of the history of this location distinguishable in the new Humboldt-Forum.

Nachkriegsplanung/Post-war planning: Gerhardt Kosel
Aus/From: Helmut Engel, Schauplatz Mitte. Berlin: Jovis Verlag 1998

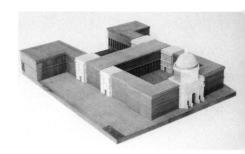

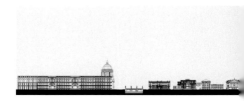

Werkverzeichnis/List of works
Auswahl Bauten, Projekte und Wettbewerbe/Selection of Buildings, Projects and Competitions

1992	Projektwettbewerb Museum des 20. Jahrhunderts, Nürnberg; Ankauf
1993	Projektwettbewerb Doppelsporthalle Rudowerstraße, Berlin-Treptow; 3. Preis
	Projektwettbewerb für die Errichtung eines Neubaus der Max-Planck-Gesellschaft mit einem städtebaulichen Ideenwettbewerb im Bereich des Marstallgeländes und des Altstadtringes, München; 1. Preis (Städtebau), 3. Preis (Realisierung)
	Gutachterverfahren Urbanisierung des ehemaligen Geländes der SS-Kaserne, Oranienburg; 2. Preis
1994	Projektwettbewerb Bildungszentrum Barnetstrasse, Berlin-Tempelhof; 3. Preis
	Städtebaulicher Ideenwettbewerb Wohnen und Arbeiten am Kanal, Seelze; 3. Preis
1	Städtebaulicher Ideenwettbewerb Otto-von-Guericke-Universität, Magdeburg; 1. Preis
	Projektwettbewerb Neubau für das Deutsche Bibliotheksinstitut, Berlin; Ankauf

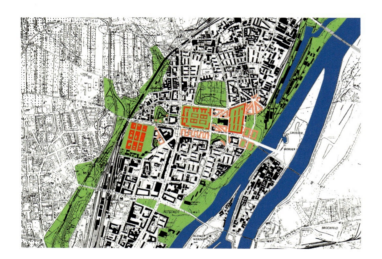

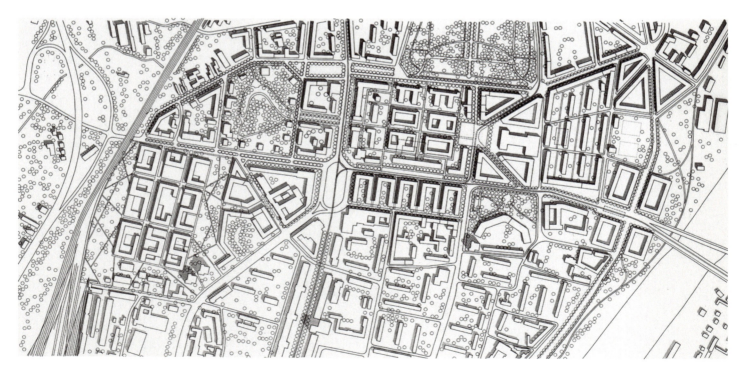

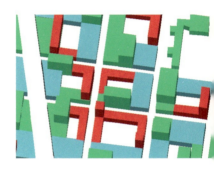
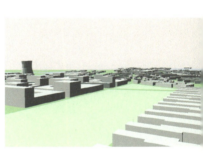
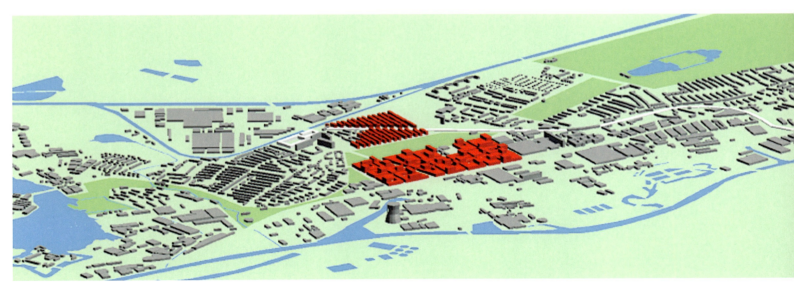

1994	**2**	Städtebaulicher Wettbewerb Nordwestliche Erweiterung der Siemensstadt, Paulsternstrasse, Berlin; 2. Preis
1996–1998		Studentenwohnheime, Brandenburg 1. Bauetappe; Realisierungswettbewerb 1995, 1. Preis
		Thermal Sole Bad Saarow, Kurpark; Realisierungswettbewerb 1995, 1. Preis
1997		Museum der Bildenden Künste, Leipzig; Realisierungswettbewerb 1997, 1. Preis
		Projektwettbewerb Kunsthaus, Graz; Preisträger
1998		Projektwettbewerb Informations- und Kommunikationszentrum Adlershof, Berlin; Ankauf
2000		Projektwettbewerb Kurbad, Meran; 2. Preis
	3	Städtebaulicher Ideenwettbewerb, Umgebung des Weimarplatzes, Weimar
2001	**4**	Projektwettbewerb Literaturmuseum der Moderne, Marbach am Neckar; Ankauf

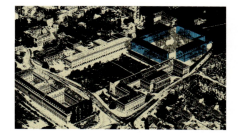  

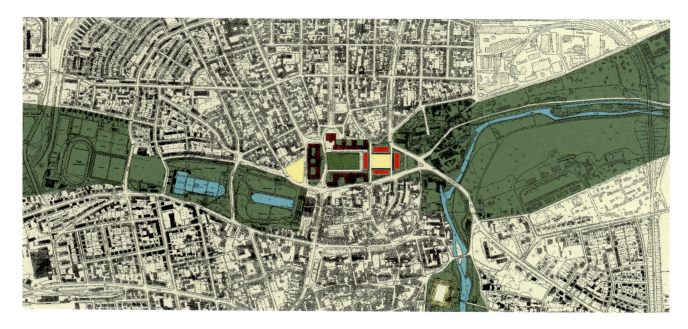

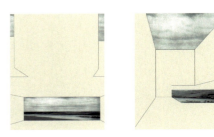

4

2001		Projektwettbewerb Freizeithallenbad beim Freibad Kallebad, Wiesbaden; 3. Preis
		Projektwettbewerb Museum für Moderne Kunst, Bozen; Anerkennung
2002	**5**	Rathaus und Gemeindezentrum, Bernried; Realisierungswettbewerb, 2. Preis
2004		Sporthalle zur Max-Taut-Schule, Berlin; Beschränkter Realisierungswettbewerb, 1. Preis
		Wettbewerb Jacob und Wilhelm Grimm-Zentrum. Zentrale Universitätsbibliothek der Humboldt-Universität, Berlin; Ankauf
2005		Wettbewerb Neubau eines Freizeitbads, Braunschweig; 2. Preis
		Städtebaulicher Ideenwettbewerb Museumshöfe, Berlin; 3. Preis
2006–2007	**6**	Realisierungswettbewerb Bundesministerium des Innern, Berlin
2009		Erweiterung der Kunsthalle, Bremen; Realisierungswettbewerb 2005, 1. Preis
2009–2010		Studentenwohnheime, Brandenburg 2. Bauetappe; Realisierungswettbewerb 1995, 1. Preis

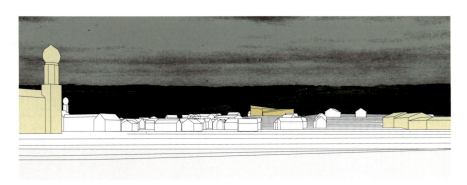

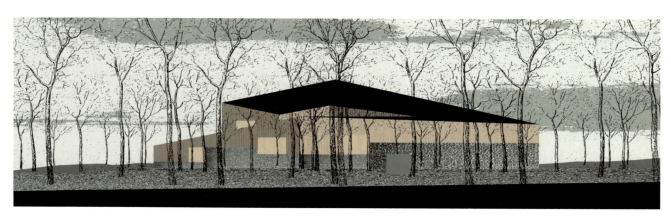

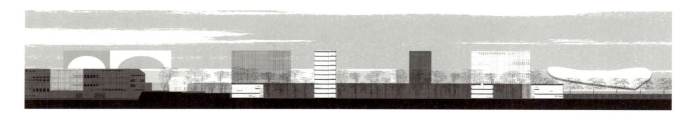

Karl Hufnagel	1958	geboren in Heidelberg
	1978–1992	Studium an der FH Wiesbaden und an der HdK Berlin
	1994	Architekturdiplom Hochschule der Künste Berlin
	1981–1983	Lehrauftrag für Baukonstruktion und Architekturdarstellung an der Fachhochschule Wiesbaden
	1983–1985	Mitarbeit bei der Internationalen Bauausstellung Berlin
	1990	Assistenz am Wiener Architekturseminar Expo Werkstatt
	1985–1993	freier Mitarbeiter in verschiedenen Büros in Berlin
	seit 1992	gemeinsames Büro mit Peter Pütz und Michael Rafaelian
	1958	Born in Heidelberg
	1978–1992	Studied at the FH Wiesbaden and the Berlin University of the Arts
	1994	Graduated with a diploma in Architecture from Berlin University of the Arts
	1981–1983	Lecturer at the RheinMain University of Applied Sciences
	1983–1985	Worked for the International Building Exhibition Berlin
	1990	Assistant at the architectural seminar in Vienna Expo Werkstatt
	1985–1993	Freelance work at different offices in Berlin
	since 1992	Architectural office together with Peter Pütz and Michael Rafaelian
Peter Pütz	1957	geboren in Mönchengladbach
	1985	Architekturdiplom Technische Universität Berlin
	1985–1990	freier Mitarbeiter in verschiedenen Büros in Berlin und Sevilla
	1990–1993	wissenschaftlicher Mitarbeiter an der Universität Dortmund, Lehrstuhl Entwerfen und Gebäudelehre
	seit 1992	gemeinsames Büro mit Karl Hufnagel und Michael Rafaelian
	1957	born in Mönchengladbach
	1985	Graduated with a diploma in Architecture from TU (technical university) Berlin
	1985–1990	Freelance work at different offices in Berlin and Seville
	1990–1993	Research Assistant at the TU University Dortmund, Lecturing post for the subjects Design and Building Theory
	since 1992	Architectural office together with Karl Hufnagel and Michael Rafaelian
Michael Rafaelian	1955	geboren in München
	1978–1990	Studium an der FH München, TFH Berlin und HdK Berlin
	1984	Architekturdiplom Hochschule der Künste Berlin
	1986–1991	Tätigkeit als freier Mitarbeiter in verschiedenen Berliner Architekturbüros mit Konzentration auf Architektur und Landschaftsarchitektur
	seit 1992	gemeinsames Büro mit Karl Hufnagel und Peter Pütz
	1955	born in Munich
	1978–1990	Studied at the FH Munich, TFH Berlin and Berlin University of the Arts
	1984	Graduated with a diploma in Architecture from Berlin University of the Arts
	1986–1991	Freelance work at different architect offices in Berlin with main focus on Architecture and Landscape Architecture
	since 1992	Architectural office together with Karl Hufnagel and Peter Pütz

Auszeichnungen/Awards	1999	Anerkennung beim Deutschen Natursteinpreis (Thermalbad Saarow)
	2003	Stahlinnovationspreis (Museum der bildenden Künste Leipzig)
		Internationaler Städtebaupreis (Museumsquartier Leipzig)
		«Architettura e Design per la Città» (Urban Center del Comune Milano)
		«Urbanistica e Casa 2003» (Comune di Bologna)
	2005	Deutscher Kritikerpreis Architektur und Städtebau
		Berufung in den Konvent für Baukultur durch die Bundesstiftung Baukultur, Potsdam

Bibliographie/Bibliography	1994	Junge Beiträge zur Architektur (Vorwort Hans Kollhoff). Wiesbaden: Nelte Verlag
	1998	Beiträge zum Museum der bildenden Künste Leipzig. In: Leipziger Blätter 32
		Studentenwohnheim Brandenburg. In: Bauwelt 33, Berlin. S. 1826–1829
		Kunsthaus Graz. In: Schweizer BauJournal 2, Küttigen AG
		Stadtreparatur mit Stadtkrone. In: Architektur Jahrbuch 1998 DAM. München: Prestel Verlag
		Museum der bildenden Künste Leipzig. In: Architektur Jahrbuch 1998 DAM. München: Prestel Verlag
		Geschichte/Aufgabe/Bauvorhaben. OBB der Stadt Leipzig (Hrsg.)
		Projekte Hufnagel Pütz Rafaelian. Merseburg: Gehrig Verlag. S. 26–30
	1999	Studentenwohnheim Brandenburg. In: wettbewerbe aktuell 1, Freiburg i. Br. S. 109–112
		Thermalbad in Bad Saarow. In: wettbewerbe aktuell, Freiburg i. Br. S. 115–118
		Leipziger Bauten 1989–1999 (Hrsg. von Ingeborg Flagge). Basel: Birkhäuser Verlag
		Thermalbad Bad Saarow. In: Bauwelt 22, Berlin. S. 1212–1219
	2001	Suitcase architecture. Bensheim: selected views Verlag
		Museum der bildenden Künste Leipzig. Beitrag von K. Hufnagel. In: Frankfurter Allgemeine Zeitung 49, Frankfurt am Main
		«Architektur, Planen, Bauen». Museum der bildenden Künste Leipzig. Beitrag von K. Hufnagel. In: Frankfurter Allgemeine Zeitung 49, Frankfurt
	2002	New Buildings & Projects. Architecture in Germany. Wiesbaden: Nelte Verlag
		Museum der bildenden Künste Leipzig. «Ein Vorhang für die Kunst». VBI März, Berlin. S. 13
		Space, Time, Architecture. Berlin: Jovis Verlag
	2003	Student dormitory by Steven Holl. world architecture 10, Bejing CN
		Rethinking. Hrsg. Bund Deutscher Architekten BDI, Berlin
		Space-Time-Architecture. A dialogue between Art and Architecture. Berlin: Jovis Verlag
	2004	Doppelsporthalle Berlin Lichtenberg. Zwischen Taut und Platte. In: Bauwelt 35, Berlin. S. 22
		«Leipzig leuchtet». In: Art 12, Hamburg
		Museum der bildenden Künste Leipzig. In: Bauwelt 46, Berlin. S. 12–21
		Kulturstiftung Leipzig. Leipziger Blätter Nr. 45
	2005	musée trouvé. A photography projekt by Jill Luise Muessig. Heidelberg: Edition Braus
		Architektur Berlin 05. Über die Vereinbarkeit von Bauen. Hrsg. Architektenkammer Berlin.
		Berlin: Verlagshaus Braun
		Architektur und Städtebau in Leipzig 2000–2015. Berlin: Verlagshaus Braun
		Moderne Monumentaliteit. In: de Architect 6, Den Haag
		«Möglichkeitsräume der Kunst». In: Werk, Bauen + Wohnen 4, Zürich
		«Un grande museo per la nuova Lipsia». In: Exporre 54, Milano
		Cornelia Dörries: Die neuen Architekturführer Nr. 62. Berlin: Stadtwandel Verlag
		Museum der bildenden Künste Seite. DAM Jahrbuch 2005. Architektur in Deutschland. München: Prestel Verlag
		Bad Saarow. Centri benessere. Milano: Federico Motta Editore

Quart Verlag Luzern/Quart Publishers Lucerne

De aedibus international
5   Tony Fretton Architects (dt/e)
4   Jonathan Woolf Architects (dt/e)
3   Hufnagel Pütz Rafaelian (dt/e)
2   Hild und K (dt/e)
1   Stanton Williams (dt/e)

De aedibus – Zeitgenössische Schweizer Architekten und ihre Bauten
Contemporary Swiss architects and their buildings
39   Atelier Bonnet (dt/e)
38   Novaron (dt/e)
37   Althammer Hochuli (dt/e)
36   Schneider & Schneider (dt/e)
35   Frei & Ehrensperger (dt und e)
34   Liechti Graf Zumsteg (dt/e)
33   Adrian Streich (dt/e)
32   Daniele Marques (dt/e)
31   Neff Neumann (dt/e)
30   Giraudi Wettstein (dt/e)
29   Steinmann & Schmid (dt/e)
28   Matthias Ackermann (dt/e)
27   Aeby & Perneger (dt/e)
26   Bakker & Blanc (dt/e)
25   Markus Wespi Jérôme de Meuron (dt/e)
24   Bauart (dt/e und dt/f)
23   Knapkiewicz & Fickert (dt/e)
22   Marcel Ferrier (dt/e)
21   Wild Bär Architekten (dt/e)
20   Enzmann + Fischer (dt/e)
19   Mierta und Kurt Lazzarini (dt/e)
18   Rolf Mühlethaler (dt/e)
17   Pablo Horváth (dt/e)
16   Brauen + Wälchli (dt/e)
15   E2A Eckert Eckert Architekten (dt/e)
14   Lussi + Halter (dt/e)
13   Philipp Brühwiler (dt/e)
12   Scheitlin – Syfrig + Partner (dt/e)
11   Vittorio Magnago Lampugnani. Stadtarchitekturen/Urban Architectures (dt/e)
10   Bonnard Woeffray. Time (dt/e und dt/f)
9   Graber Pulver. Werkstücke/Workpieces (dt/e)
8   Burkhalter Sumi/Makiol Wiederkehr. Konstruktionen/Constructions (dt/e)
7   Gigon/Guyer. Projekte (dt und e)
6   Andrea Bassi. Figuren (dt, f und e)
5   Dieter Jüngling und Andreas Hagmann. Bauwerke (dt und e)
4   Beat Consoni. Fünf Arbeiten (dt und e)
3   Max Bosshard & Christoph Luchsinger. Abdruck Ausdruck (dt)
2   Miroslav Šik. Altneu (dt, e und i)
1   Valentin Bearth & Andrea Deplazes. Räumlinge (dt, e und i)

Monografien/Monographs
Valerio Olgiati (dt und e)
Burkard Meyer. Konkret/Concrete (dt/e)
Gion A. Caminada. Cul zuffel e l'aura dado (dt/e)

Quart Verlag GmbH, Heinz Wirz; Verlag für Architektur und Kunst
Denkmalstrasse 2, CH-6006 Luzern; books@quart.ch, www.quart.ch